T0209149

RHYMES
TO REPROGRAM
YOUR SUBCONSCIOUS MIND

RHYMES
TO REPROGRAM
YOUR SUBCONSCIOUS MIND

"HEAL DEEP TRAUMA
BECOME YOUR GREATEST VERSION"
"MASTER YOURSELF MASTER YOUR WORLD"

NARIAH WEBSTER

RHYMES TO REPROGRAM YOUR SUBCONSCIOUS MIND
"HEAL DEEP TRAUMA BECOME YOUR GREATEST VERSION"
"MASTER YOURSELF MASTER YOUR WORLD"

iUniverse books may be ordered through booksellers or by contacting:

iUniverse
1663 Liberty Drive
Bloomington, IN 47403
www.iuniverse.com
844-349-9409

Because of the dynamic nature of the Internet, any web addresses or links contained in this book may have changed since publication and may no longer be valid. The views expressed in this work are solely those of the author and do not necessarily reflect the views of the publisher, and the publisher hereby disclaims any responsibility for them.

Any people depicted in stock imagery provided by Getty Images are models, and such images are being used for illustrative purposes only. Certain stock imagery © Getty Images.

ISBN: 978-1-6632-5787-1 (sc)
ISBN: 978-1-6632-5786-4 (hc)
ISBN: 978-1-6632-5788-8 (e)

Library of Congress Control Number: 2023921546

Print information available on the last page.

iUniverse rev. date: 11/13/2023

ACKNOWLEDGMENTS

I'm thankful for my friends and family: Mark Hicks; Matthew, the Mac, you taught me how to take my power back; Max, for assisting me to maximize my potential; "Nothing that was Done cannot be Undone" (Ja Emmanuel); Diane Shepard; Willie Webster; Nicholas Webster; Lisa Nichols; Natasha Marie; my nephews Remirez and Romeiro; Michele Baena; Kristin Andreocci; Shon Johnson (Pooh); Shondraya (Kennedy); Annie and the kids; Denise; Kristina Monk Temple; the Elliott family; Detroit family and friends; the Village Studios; G-Carlo; Javoe; Sophie, aka IAMBIGSOPH; GA family and friends; Lyndon; Raleigh, you helped me tap into my creativity; Shout Out The Salonde Weave Team; Weavemaster; H. R. S.; Capo; Mikie; ey3visionfilmsvfx,BossMan/BossBusinesss, Inc.; E. I.; Ley; D; BJ, you shined on me like the sunray; Niquise, for gratitude is to be released; Vonshey, I love you, though you got on my nerves times 222! Vari, till infinity and beyond the end, you taught me how to earth bend. LingoLive, you kept my spirit alive. Doelow, you kept me on my mission when I was down and solo! Tashawn the Great, you showed me I had what it takes.

INTRODUCTION

Ready, set, Empress, empower us! The space of God goes beyond the laws of physics. The space of God has the ability to beat all odds. The I am is far beyond definition!

Most breakthroughs rely on subtraction instead of addition. In a material world, we're always seeking things we can add. How about trying to think about what we can subtract? Yes, it's time to get naked! You begin to take off the false identities you made up about yourself and chose to identify with, thereby giving them power. You eventually come to realize that having a false identity and label is nothing special as everyone has them. Collectively, we give things power—images, objects, names, and so on. We label millionaires as millionaires when, in reality, that's all they know to be; they don't know how to act like anyone or anything else. Do you see the difference? Being vs. acting. Do you think that God acts like God or simply just is?

Regardless of whether people argue, debate, fight, or disagree about something's existence or nonexistence, at the end of the day, it simply just is. Fun fact: When God gives you a gift, everyone is not going to have the same gift.

Getting to know the real you—your core being—by remembering your inner being takes a bit more practice in shedding that outdated cocoon.

You can now give yourself permission to step into your true inner being. You don't have to act anymore. That's what Hollywood is for.

It's time to shut off your mind and think with your heart. Now, let's take a journey back in time. It's OK to talk to your soul: "Hey soul, guide me to the ability to see God of all infinite possibilities appropriate to solutions to all things that assist my ascension and that of and humankind."

Following are some definitions to know:

> *Infinite possibilities:* Having no limits or boundaries in time, space, extent, or magnitude. It means possessing the mindset that anything can happen within and beyond the fabric of reality.

> *Ascension:* The act of rising to an important position or a higher level.

> *Solution:* An action or process of solving a problem; an answer to a problem.

It is helpful to have a personal mission statement. Mine is, "Empower, and profits will follow." If you have a company, create a slogan that inspires you and encourages faith and belief in you with clients or customers. Mine is, "Dream big or go dig."

Each business should have a plan that reflects its ideology. I use the Riah business formula: RD + RQS = C. Expressed another way, relevant demand + reliable quality supply = cash flow. My long-term goal is to inspire like minds, design a program teaching a billion people how to make $48,000 to $80,000 a year doing something they are gifted at, born to do, and love. I hope to expand enough to create more than 144 millionaires across the globe.

Before all things—literally *all* things, including language. Yes, even including language, which is just ways of articulation and identification. Before rulership, taxes, hierarchies of the world. Fun fact: 70 to 93 percent of all communication is nonverbal. Even Google will tell you that.

OK, carrying on. Yes, before business, politics, religion, entertainment, duality, equality, karma, drama, fear, energy, emotion, reality, yin and yang, jobs, money. And science, which is only the discovery and utilization of things *already here*. Otherwise, there would be nothing without original substance to study from. Before all these things came to be, there was something beyond what humans could comprehend with only what they could see. Some call it God, which is the divine link to all possibilities.

What is fear? It's just false evidence that appears to be real. The soul nature is not fear. Therefore, fear is more likely the indoctrination of human emotions. The root of emotion is really the energy you choose to allow to move. When you stop energy in motion, you weaken your practice. So how do we make things stop? You stop energy in motion by being still. You become aware what you choose to give attention to—give energy to—and to then decide what to do next.

You're almost there. To be still is to become aware.

God can shapeshift in all things, whether it be in silence, a word, thought, dream, person, place, animal, air, fire, water, earth, or thing. Mind-blowing, I know!

A true star must learn to master his or her avatar. In this world, we're always trying to define things with our egos. We're also trying to get somewhere only to realize we're already where we are trying to get to. For example, everything you're looking for in someone is an observation of what's in you. The more you get in tune with what's best for you, the more you'll attract (as in having the necessary sight, discernment, and level of awareness) by vibrating in the essence of your alignment an identify with those who are there to highlight and bring out the best in you. Why? Because you made the choice to want to bring out the best in yourself. Otherwise, how would you have made it this far? It starts within you. Thus, the nature of the birth of creation. Just like a baby, an idea that started as just a thought can be born into the form of what we call reality.

Do People and Things Really Die?

Or do they return to their original states and evolve? Well, evolution is nature, and change is inevitable. Tap into common sense; common sense is nature. For example, nature is information. When an apple falls off a tree and sits on the ground for a while, some call it diseased, expired, and rotten. But in actuality, the apple is feeding the earth's soil as it returns to its original state. I'll leave that one up to you to discern and decide!

Self-Realization:
Where Hurt Comes From

Hurt comes from hiding. Once you're able to observe what you're hiding from, get quiet, so you can hear God and simply allow the truth to set you free. What is truth linked to? Wisdom, which is the application of knowledge. What happens when you know better? You do better!

Yay! Getting quiet so you can hear God is like clicking on the link to gain access to all possibilities and solutions. Always stay focused on what gives you access to solutions rather than to limitations. The only way to do this is to expand your awareness to identify God. The soul always knows best! Now, let's take a leap out of the nest!

Eight Laws to Remember

1. Karma can become liberating through the power of transmutation.
2. Transmutation is developed by ascension. When ascension and transmutation collide, it becomes a resurrection. As in the new birth of a transformation of one being reborn, made original.
3. Ascension is formed by a solid, conscious decision. Interpret what this decision is for you. Your soul knows.
4. Decisions in the now determine the future. Some relate this as the butterfly effect in the sense that small things often have huge impacts.
5. Rise above the fear of settling by paying attention to the intent you're setting. Yes, this includes in every setting !
6. What is for you, you can create to make run toward you! In other words, be what you want to attract. Be yourself; become one with the greatest version of yourself. You can attract your soulmate by simply being your soul's mate. Become one with self, and you will birth something great!
7. Become the master observer.
8. Become the product of the worlds you create to collide.

VERSE 111

Sit back, relax, and pull over. I know you might feel like you've been hit by a bulldozer,
but trust me, my baby, your life is not over.

Focus on your strengths, and you will go the length.
You are not broken; you are a token.

Let your focus not be on weak. It is now time to lead by taking that leap of faith.
Put your trust in not what you can see. Tell yourself, "Nobody was born me."

Competition? There is no need to compete.
You are complete. Don't you know it is your birthright to be free?

Do not feel because you are a little gray that you cannot begin a brand-new day.
You will be OK!

So what if the skies are a little gray?
Rise from hypnotize, lift the veil off your eyes, see that you are the prize.
Come alive and strive.

We need you! You have the ability to impact lives by being you!
By the way, when you're at the top, let me know, "How is the view?"
Appreciate all that you have had and will accumulate.

VERSE 222

Your world is a divine design created by your own mind.
Dig deeper into the mine.
There's much more than just coal to find.
You will discover gold unrefined.

Dear divine, what will you decide to do with this time, lie in your bed and cast away?
Get up!

Screw your mood!
Always allow action to be the move, and you will never lose.
Soon you will see that the lack of energy was just another enemy!

VERSE 333

Get ready for the hot seat!
Don't you know that every no
is an opportunity to grow?
All these rules and regulations
are just other forms of temptation.
Where there's resilience,
there lies brilliance.
Today's lesson is self-reflection.
See beyond the illusion of what you call rejection!

VERSE 444

Life is like a university rehab facility of anything: Too much, and to kill
you, it has the ability.
Balance is key.
Change is not your enemy.
Embrace the inevitable, and you will go beyond capacity.
It's as simple as one and two creates three.
Stagnant was never our nature, you see.
From day 1, we were born from creativity.

VERSE 555

Built-up confrontation may cause lack of concentration.
The frustration may drive you to feel a tense sensation, as if suddenly, you
have the adrenaline to hop over the fence.
But if you could hold on just a little while longer off the defense,
everything will soon start to make sense.
Patience is the cure to negligence.

VERSE 666

Learning from mistakes only teaches you that you've got what it takes!
Time to take a break from the ringing of the phone,
and you will bear the beauty of being alone.
You get to set your own tone.

~ ~ ~ ~

VERSE 777

Every day you can be made brand new.
It is yourself—you—should be trying to outdo!
Your mind?
Yes, you tell it what to do!
Amid any disaster, remember you are your mind's master.

~ ~ ~ ~

VERSE 888

We all fail, but to dwell on our fails is like voluntarily locking yourself
inside a cell.
Just do it like Nike, and you will prevail.
Open the doors,
and victory is yours!
Unworthy excuse me objection.
Never fear rejection.
Learning is repetition; consistency is key.
Opportunity is preparation; preparation meets opportunity.

VERSE 999

Where there is guilt lies an opportunity for you to be rebuilt.
Use your intuition,
and next time, make wise your decision!
How can you overcome the temptation of the day?
By setting your intention without further delay!

VERSE 1010

Were you struggling to hold steadfast?
Did you start to move too fast and reminisced about the past?
Dear relapse, you can relax
for we shall rebuild that which cannot collapse!

VERSE 1111

Dear free will,
learn to be still.
Before you conclude to make a move,
I set before you life or death; you choose.
Destruct or develop? How about an upgrade, becoming self-made
into something new,
choosing the pathway of only a few?

VERSE 1212

Life is choice driven by you!
Use the power of the observer, and choose what to take.
Would you like icing along with your cake?
Never settle ... double take
for you may be making a big mistake.

VERSE 1313

Success leaves cheat codes.
Be ready to act, and watch it all unfold!

VERSE 1414

How is your attitude?
This will define your latitude.
There's always room to improve.
Use gratitude to identify your gifts, which in divine time,
is designed to make room for you.
In this moment, reflect on your mood, move,
and choose to dance to a new groove.
Eliminate resistance;
replace it with resilience.
Proceed with persistence,
and you will go the distance.

VERSE 1515

Rest empty your mind to renew,
and do what is *best* for you.
Everything is fine;
you are free to unwind.
The beauty of the pursuit, to pursue,
is to keep on doing what you desire to do.
Realize in due time being you has value.
The work you do definitely adore,
but realize you have the power to do more!

VERSE 1616

Without further delay,
today is the day you come a long way.
Practice persistence, and it will be given.
Here's an equation to the top of the tower:
Knowledge applied equals power!

VERSE 1717

Destined from birth
to the meek, who shall inherit the earth,
all that you seek is already a given.
Take the wheel and keep driven.
This is not the end; keep strivin'!
To free yourself from condemnation,
just go within, and have a conversation.

VERSE 1818

There's no time for snoozing.
Never feel as though you're losing for the art of winning is to keep moving!
Realize that you're awesome,
and the world is ready for you to blossom!

VERSE 1919

Apart from the rest, realize you are unique and increased.
You are to go after your destiny
with so much tenacity.
We are not to be in fear, held in captivity,
but loved, adored, active, adaptive, innovative, creative,
free to be expressive,
at peace and ease, swimming in pools of ecstasy.
Find what is radiating to thee,
and that will be key.
"Put fire onto your desire, channel the power that self-love possesses
to pave the way for your successes.
Glorify the nature of your divine design to free your mind.
We are to use but not Abuse our gifts to uplift!
Spread love
by being a reflection of that from above!"
For you are a divine design.
You've always been at the finish line.
So, therefore, what race?
That which is unserving to you, you are to erase and allow space at the perfect
pace to be the case!
Be busy being great.
It's time to make the world quake!

VERSE 2020

All things are consumed in the mind first, before it can be given birth.

VERSE 2121

If its cause is distress, may be put to rest after you've done all that you could
do, and said all that you can say.
If it is a burden, may it be lay as we are bombarded throughout the day.
It's OK if you've gone astray;
just come back without delay!
If it's done no good deed, it has no purpose to proceed!
Lack? Excuse me, what is that? The devil, how clever.
You are never in need.
You will always be provided with plenty indeed!

VERSE 2222

Ego death today as if it's your last breath.
Give good gifts to uplift,
never forcing, always flowing.
As you've planted a good deed, the seed has been sewn.
Now let it grow and be left alone until it is grown!
The work is done; be patient and proceed.

VERSE 2323

Guard your speech so that it may be sweet
for you attract what you speak.
Therefore, speak from a place of integrity and purity!

VERSE 2424

Victim tears,
it's time to face your fears!
Witness the beauty of intimacy by choosing to go inside and see!
Soul, it's not fearful; take responsibility, and free your mentality!
Consistency and repetition will be the key.
Daily respond to the power of the cosmos; allow the energy to flow
from head, shoulders, knees to your toes!
Create rather than compete; let that be how it goes.
If it is success that you desire, will let it be required.
Don't shame it.
Claim it!

VERSE 2525

The truth of losing your mind
is that sometimes, you must lose in order to find
the realization it's time to go inside your soul and entwine to unwind.
Discovered from this process a priceless gold,
which can never be sold.
Where there's resistance, release it, and let it flow.

VERSE 2626

There is power in saying no.
If it is toxic, as you know,
is time to let it go,
so that you can flow.
For change is inevitable, and to elevate
is the only gate.

VERSE 2727

Unlock those chains for a change.
Learn to embrace change!

VERSE 2828

Thoughts of poverty still your sovereignty,
eliminate scarcity for the world is abundant and has plenty of property.
The search for security is an illusion called insecurity.
Striving for success?
Time to pop out the nest
for the uncomfortability of uncertainty
is the creative key!

VERSE 2929

You need not to be an inquisition.
Rise to what is given.
Just do you, no questions.
Stop asking for permission
to claim your position.

VERSE 3030

Choose to live uprightly,

with a sober mind and gratitude as the key.

You are free from iniquity, immediately removed from negativity,

and the cleansing of your energy,

so you are receptive to current opportunity.

Open your eyes, and you will see!

~ ~ ~ ~

VERSE 3131

Sometimes we all get lost in the sauce.

Do not be fooled by the hype as the rest drool.

Just do you and the work you set out to do.

Complete the mission with tunnel vision.

God is not the author of confusion.

Simplify your life; that is conclusion.

If it causes friction,

let it go without jurisdiction.

~ ~ ~ ~

VERSE 3232

What seeds have you begun to breed?
What books have you begun to read?
What kingdoms have you begun to lead?
If approaching were your last days, what new ways are you to pave
before the grave?
What story are you telling?
What expectations are you intending?
What intentions are you sending?
What goals have you left pending?
What legacy do you plan on leaving?
Self-reflect and take a step back.
Be the observer of your canvas for we are all born from history
as artists to create and cultivate in a world of mystery!

VERSE 3333

Where the heart is, is where lies the key.
Where the sky is, is what lies beneath!
To inherit is the destiny of the meek.
Limitless, aren't we?
And this is the retreat where we are meant to be
prosperous, swimming in pools of plenty!

VERSE 3434

Enjoy your estate, but make no mistake and underestimate that you're great.
Every day you can pave a brand-new way, create a brand-new wave, innovate a brand-new phase.

*****

VERSE 3535

Sometimes we lose sight.
But it's only in our darkest moments that we discover our greatest light.

*****

VERSE 3636

That which you do not hate, you will tolerate.
Learn how to say no
so that your cup can overflow!

/ / / /

VERSE 3737

When in doubt,
gratitude will bail you out.

/ / / /

VERSE 3838

Self-control is muscle that, when applied, has the power of a missile.
Build it strong,
and you will go long.

~ ~ ~ ~

VERSE 3939

Want to do something new?
Start by adding value to those amongst you.

~ ~ ~ ~

VERSE 4040

To be observant without judgment is key to mind silence!

VERSE 4141

Growth lies where comfortability dies.

VERSE 4242

Change is a persistent, disintegrative resistance
renewing your mind to go the distance.
Stay content with consistence!

* * * * *

VERSE 4343

Rise and shine!
I believe it's about that time to grind.

* * * * *

VERSE 4444

Life is like a game we all have no choice but to play.
Temptations may come along every day,
but you have the power to choose your way.

VERSE 4545

Even amid the chaos,
eliminate all thoughts of loss.
Everything will be okay.
An increase of prosperity is on its way!

VERSE 4646

Remember: You're the prize.
Discouragement is only an opportunity to access courage in disguise.

VERSE 4747

If it doesn't flow, don't go.
But if it's in motion,
get on the boat, and ride the ocean.

VERSE 4848

What is gravity without force?
A jockey is needed to guide a wild horse.
And sometimes we must take hold of the reins to move relentlessly along
the course!

~ ~ ~ ~

VERSE 4949

Here's a clue to staying true to you:
Accepting full responsibility of the present moment will do.

~ ~ ~ ~

VERSE 5050

Different results require different approaches!

VERSE 5151

Take some time to unwind and practice silence in the mind.
You already have what it takes to shine; you already have what you need
to succeed.
Gratitude applied is key.
You just need to see that God is in you literally!
Go with and resume;
the Almighty is waiting for you to tap in tune.
God will tell you which way to go
for you are already powerful, more than you know.
Set your attention to planting seeds of positivity.
And what will blossom is an abundance of opportunities
for, I repeat, gratitude is key.
Start now, and plant new seeds.

VERSE 5252

Wherever your focus goes, energy grows.

VERSE 5353

Never force, but go with the flow.
If you are stuck on which way to go,
it's okay to be still until you know.

VERSE 5454

If it's coming from the ego, let God flow, and just let go.

~ ~ ~ ~

VERSE 5555

I am not a victim of my past, for the present is a gift that I have.

~ ~ ~ ~

VERSE 5656

An opportunity to protect your energy!
Tis the season to practice saying no without feeling obligated to give a
reason.

VERSE 5757

Seek your divine identity of divinity.
Limits don't exist is what
you'll see persist!

VERSE 5858

Once it's in the mental,
it's only a matter of time before it makes it to the physical.

VERSE 5959

God is coming to increase you in your season.
Everything happens for a reason.
The god in you is coming to increase you
and give you a clue of what next to do.

VERSE 6060

Boastful you don't have to be.

For one who is low-key is the possessor of God's divinity.

As you mold your dream,

keep it unseen.

May your success sneak upon all those who are oppressed.

VERSE 6161

It takes more energy to give in to the negativity.

This is proven scientifically,

so why not embrace positivity?

For one positive thought can realign the course of the whole day

just in the moment you thought you were going astray.

VERSE 6262

Seek for simplicity, and discover increase intensively.
You are to act accordingly
for how you act is what you will attract.

✓ ✓ ✓ ✓

VERSE 6363

To be a genius: Divide the word *genius,* and you will discover the *geni[e]*
in us.

✓ ✓ ✓ ✓

VERSE 6464

The present is literally a present! Keep unwrapping, and the rest will unfold.

Boom!

You just discovered gold!

VERSE 6565

Look for love within the now and here versus later and elsewhere!

VERSE 6666

Hold your horses!
Seek inside, and you'll find unlimited resources.

✔ ✔ ✔ ✔

VERSE 6767

Contentment is found in acceptance of the present moment.

✔ ✔ ✔ ✔

VERSE 6868

Time for a backbone.
Get out of your comfort zone!

VERSE 6969

Watch what you give energy to, especially when it's not true.

VERSE 7070

Riches is to realize, to follow your life path.
That which is simple will make you the most math.
If it isn't adding up,
it's tearing down your luck.

VERSE 7171

When you don't give up and instead proceed,
it guarantees you will succeed.
Just believe!

VERSE 7272

Get hip when you see a synchronicity glitch in this matrix. God certainly exists in symbols and mathematics!

ﾉ ﾉ ﾉ ﾉ

VERSE 7373

Are you being controlling, or are you taking control of your being?

ﾉ ﾉ ﾉ ﾉ

VERSE 7474

Happiness can be built in stillness.
Patience builds resilience.

~ ~ ~ ~

VERSE 7575

All things can be solved from within you. The world revolves around the
real you, not the ego you flee to.

~ ~ ~ ~

VERSE 7676

Fear is the creation of false evidence created in the imagination. Proceed with purpose.

VERSE 7777

To have patience, feel the sensation of the present as the destination!

VERSE 7878

Energy is the greatest form of currency.

VERSE 7979

Don't give fear the privilege to cause commotion.
Place aside all fears, and put courage in motion!

VERSE 8080

The faster you fail,
the quicker you shall prevail!

VERSE 8181

If you want someone else to change, look in the mirror, and first take off
your chains!

VERSE 8282

When one door is closed, another unfolds.

VERSE 8383

Begin in the essence by tapping into the sensi of your senses.

VERSE 8484

Pr-ayer: Pr—practice element air.

*****

VERSE 8585

Let go of the past tense, and grasp the beauty of the present presence of your true essence!

*****

VERSE 8686

To finish is to leave behind that which is diminished.
To finish is to begin again and replenish!

VERSE 8787

What God has for you is not going anywhere.
Trust the process, and you will surely make it there.
Look a little closer if you dare.
Be bold enough to receive what is already there.

VERSE 8888

Do what you must do.

Do what you want to do.

Do it for you.

Do it for them too.

Do it now, and do it then.

Do it again, and then ascend.

～～～～

VERSE 8989

Time to step up to the booth and walk in your truth.

Realize you never had to sacrifice.

See, but not with your own eyes, every loss was a divine gain in disguise.

～～～～

VERSE 9090

Do the work that can be done today in an efficient way!

~ ~ ~ ~

VERSE 9191

Come face-to-face.
Embrace what you are trying to escape.
Hold off no longer for it will make you stronger.

~ ~ ~ ~

VERSE 9292

Let love, and let go!

VERSE 9393

Where energy goes
is that which grows.

VERSE 9494

Feel that which you want to channel.

/ / / /

VERSE 9595

Become just that; be that which you want to attract.
Do this, and you will Find your match.
Those who dare to dream deserve a better scene:
To embrace the blessings of that which was unseen.

/ / / /

VERSE 9696

Feel like you're losing?
Embrace growth, then keep it moving.
Release from the physical.
Be intentional with your actions.
Allow them to be radical.

VERSE 9797

Why settle when change is inevitable?

VERSE 9898

A wake-up call for all:
Look down, and see the time is now!
The shackles on your feet have been released.

~ ~ ~ ~

VERSE 9999

The moment we begin to overcomplicate is the moment to separate.

~ ~ ~ ~

VERSE 1000

Purpose will be identified.
For right now, enjoy the present ride.

VERSE 1002

Break free from scarcity belief.
Know your worth by embracing a new mentality.
Realize you have plenty.
Who you are is just enough substance to create a brand-new reality.

VERSE 1003

There is no losing.
There's only growing and keeping it moving.

VERSE 1004

Accept the reality by realizing you create it from within thee.

VERSE 1005

Forget being lazy.
It's time to be bold and go brazy.

VERSE 1006

You don't have to make your to-do a list
when you choose to do in the present tense.

VERSE 1007

Trust that God will straighten your route.
Have no doubt, even the wrong way has a way out.

~ ~ ~ ~

VERSE 1008

When you lay your heart on the line,
and you feel it's been declined,
take some time to renew your mind.
Focus solely on the limitless abundance of supply available to you to draw
nigh.

~ ~ ~ ~

VERSE 1009

Address your focus on everything limitless.

VERSE 1010

As you are climbing the tower,
Know the essence of speech power.
Good things into existence you are to speak.
There's power in practicing what you preach.

VERSE 1,011

Now that you know you have a purpose and destiny, what will you do to paint your reality anew?

/ / / /

VERSE 1012

Tapping into the essence of your God, that's how you beat the odds!

/ / / /

VERSE 1013

The intention you are setting is creating your setting.

VERSE 1015

Why settle when you can put more pressure on the pedal?

VERSE 1016

Push through the durations of frustrations. What will appear is a direction that is clear!

~~~~

VERSE 1017

Truth cannot be denied.
It can only be recognized.

~~~~

VERSE 1018

Master the art of how you feel.
It will reveal what is real.

VERSE 1019

There is no better time than now indeed.
You will always have what you need to proceed.

VERSE 1020

Remember your why.
This is how you can strive.
Continue to progress.
Accept nothing less.
It is yourself you should be trying to impress.

VERSE 1021

The search for security is an illusion of insecurity. True security is reflected from within for the results of what's within determine the outcome of what's without.

VERSE 1022

Be a conqueror rather than a complainer.

VERSE 1023

Salvation comes from self.
If you're gonna have temptation,
let it be for liberation!

VERSE 1024

You go 0 to 100 real quick when you don't quit!

～ ～ ～ ～

VERSE 1025

... 1 + 0 + 2 + 5 = 8.
The number 8 symbolizes practicality, karma.
Spiritual, along with the material worlds collide, and infinite possibilities
are born.

To be in a different mode,
You must learn to break codes.
It's time to drive versus being the road.
It's blueprint season.
In all we do, we do with reason—
all facts, no treason.

It's time to get rich for real!

Step out of the roles, tap into reality.
Step back to see,
and the bigger picture will come to be.

～ ～ ～ ～

VERSE 1026

... 1 + 0 + 2 + 6 = 9.
The number 9 symbolizes alpha and omega, new beginnings and endings!
Peace and harmony will be restored.
May victory be declared as yours!

Favored by the cosmos, protected by the angels,
may you simply be increased along with your endeavors.
For all things are working in your greatest favor.
A beginning and an end are for a reason,
for everything has a season.
This is the part where it gets annoying.
You must keep going for what you've done
is only a representation of what's just begun!

END OF BOOK BONUS

It really helped me on my journey to get still through silence in the present moment. I also discovered my life path number was 7, and my destiny number was 8. Knowing these things reminded me of my why, how to not allow my weaknesses to define me and being confident with identifying and applying my inner strengths! Following is a numerology frequency vibration calendar that may help assist you on your journey. Math is life. Literally!

Daily Numerology Frequency Vibration Calendar

1 —	2 二	3 三	4 四	5 五	6 六	7 七
CONFIDENCE FREEDOM POWER INDEPENDENCE CONFIDENCE LEADERSHIP ONE WITH SELF APPLYING NEW IDEAS	PEACE & POWER GRACE COMPANIONSHIP HARMONY BALANCE YIN/YANG POLARITY / DUALITY	CREATIVITY INSPIRATION COMMUNICATION ENTHUSIASM SOCIAL SKILLS HIGH POSITIVE ENERGY JOY & LAUGHTER	DISCIPLINE PRACTICALITY STABILITY RULERSHIP AUTHORITY ORGANIZATION	ENTERTAINMENT FREEDOM TRAVEL PROSPERITY JUSTICE KNOWLEDGE PURITY FREE-SPIRIT CHANGE PROGRESS 5-STAR	HOME FAMILY NURTURING SOUL SUPPORT SERVICE HEALING EMPATHY UNCONDITIONAL LOVE TEND TO THE SOUL	CLAIRVOYANCE SPIRITUAL INTELLECT WISDOM SEEKER PERFECTION LEARNING ASCENSION CURIOUS TRANSCENDING DIVING DEEP WITHIN
8 八	**9 九**	**10 (1-0-1)**	**11 (1-1-2)**	**12 (1-2-3)**	**13 (1-3-4)**	**14 (1-4-5)**
CONFIDENT SOCIAL CHALLENGER INFINITY MONEY ALL POSSIBILITIES COMPETITIVE STRENGTH GO GETTER WISDOM POWER AUTHORITY PROFESSIONAL	COMPLETION LOYALTY BOTH ENDINGS AND BEGINNINGS ADAPTIVITY ESTABLISHING PEACE	CONFIDENCE FREEDOM POWER INDEPENDENCE CONFIDENCE LEADERSHIP ONE WITH SELF APPLYING NEW IDEAS	MANIFESTATION PEACE & POWER INNER STRENGTH COMPANIONSHIP HARMONY GRACE BALANCE YIN/YANG POLARITY / DUALITY	CREATIVITY INSPIRATION COMMUNICATION ENTHUSIASM SOCIAL SKILLS HIGH POSITIVE ENERGY JOY & LAUGHTER	DISCIPLINE PRACTICALITY STABILITY RULERSHIP AUTHORITY ORGANIZATION	ENTERTAINMENT FREEDOM TRAVEL PROSPERITY JUSTICE KNOWLEDGE PURITY FREE-SPIRIT CHANGE PROGRESS 5-STAR
15 (1-5-6)	**16 (1-6-7)**	**17 (1-7-8)**	**18 (1-8-9)**	**19 (1-9-10-1)**	**20 (2-0-2)**	**21 (2-1-3)**
HOME FAMILY NURTURING SOUL SUPPORT SERVICE HEALING EMPATHY UNCONDITIONAL LOVE TEND TO THE SOUL	CLAIRVOYANCE SPIRITUAL INTELLECT WISDOM SEEKER PERFECTION LEARNING ASCENSION CURIOUS TRANSCENDING DIVING DEEP WITHIN	CONFIDENT SOCIAL CHALLENGER INFINITY MONEY ALL POSSIBILITIES COMPETITIVE STRENGTH GO GETTER WISDOM POWER AUTHORITY PROFESSIONAL	COMPLETION LOYALTY BOTH ENDINGS AND BEGINNINGS ADAPTIVITY ESTABLISHING PEACE	CONFIDENCE FREEDOM POWER INDEPENDENCE CONFIDENCE LEADERSHIP ONE WITH SELF APPLYING NEW IDEAS	PEACE & POWER GRACE COMPANIONSHIP HARMONY BALANCE YIN/YANG POLARITY / DUALITY	CREATIVITY INSPIRATION COMMUNICATION ENTHUSIASM SOCIAL SKILLS HIGH POSITIVE ENERGY JOY & LAUGHTER
22 (2-2-4)	**23 (2-3-5)**	**24 (2-4-6)**	**25 (2-5-7)**	**26 (2-6-8)**	**27 (2-7-9)**	**28 (2-8-10-1)**
EXPERT DISCIPLINE PRACTICALITY STABILITY RULERSHIP AUTHORITY ORGANIZATION	ENTERTAINMENT FREEDOM TRAVEL PROSPERITY JUSTICE KNOWLEDGE PURITY FREE-SPIRIT CHANGE PROGRESS 5-STAR	HOME FAMILY NURTURING SOUL SUPPORT SERVICE HEALING EMPATHY UNCONDITIONAL LOVE TEND TO THE SOUL	CLAIRVOYANCE SPIRITUAL INTELLECT WISDOM SEEKER PERFECTION LEARNING ASCENSION CURIOUS TRANSCENDING DIVING DEEP WITHIN	CONFIDENT SOCIAL CHALLENGER INFINITY MONEY ALL POSSIBILITIES COMPETITIVE STRENGTH GO GETTER WISDOM POWER AUTHORITY PROFESSIONAL	COMPLETION LOYALTY BOTH ENDINGS AND BEGINNINGS ADAPTIVITY ESTABLISHING PEACE	CONFIDENCE FREEDOM POWER INDEPENDENCE CONFIDENCE LEADERSHIP ONE WITH SELF APPLYING NEW IDEAS
29 (2-9-11-2)	**30 (3-0-3)**	**31 (3-1-4)**	Knowledge	Applied	is	Power !
PEACE & POWER GRACE COMPANIONSHIP HARMONY BALANCE YIN/YANG POLARITY / DUALITY	CREATIVITY INSPIRATION COMMUNICATION ENTHUSIASM SOCIAL SKILLS HIGH POSITIVE ENERGY JOY & LAUGHTER	DISCIPLINE PRACTICALITY STABILITY RULERSHIP AUTHORITY ORGANIZATION				

This is not up for debate. The purpose of having religion should be for us to find ways to relate. The mysteries of the divine one we seek require much more than a quantum leap to lead by vessel examples and demonstrate that 1 is needed by 2 to make 3! Unity is the master key. No one does it alone. Don't you see great things surely do come unto those who believe?

Stillness in the present moment and active breathwork are very helpful, along with numerology, which is the study of how numbers correlate to everyday life. To keep it simple, math is in everything we do. Literally! You can find out yours by googling "life path number calculator."

Also, I am aware of my inner vibration and the words I speak to myself. I learned very quickly that the energy within me reflected my outside reality and what I was attracting to me. I learned to declutter the chatter and think from a clearer space using my intelligence, which is more effective than just the mind alone. Most people do not know that the mind and intelligence are separate concepts. One must learn to be the master of one's mind. This can be accomplished by using the power of your intelligence, which is linked to the soul, subconscious, and invisible senses. What I found the most effective was pure silence because it helped me to tap into my soul to guide me rather than to rely on man or anything man-made. The purpose is one seeking the space where God is, which will always and forever be for eternity.

You are now feeling my genius.
As the artist, I just paint the canvas.
The interpretation is left to the mirror reflection of thy will.
If there's no enemy within, there's no enemy without.
May your pathways be clear of all fears and doubts.
God's Word has no limitations and is more than merely words on pieces of paper.
As we refer to the Word of God, go back and beyond where it all started. Who sent you here, why, and where are you to return? God's word has no bounds and is beyond the naked eye.
God's Word is far beyond what one calls words and languages.
People fear what they do not understand: fear is *false evidence appearing real*. Just remember that *soul is not fearful*, and a true leader will always point you back to yourself!

Utilizing Pr-ayer: *Pr—Practice, Ayer—Air,*
Which I Like to Refer to As the Practice of Element Air

This is one understanding of the power of utilizing your intellect; the element air is linked to intellect. To break it into simpler terms, air is invisible energy to the naked eye. Proceeding with ideas, and it pops up as a thought bubble first before it hits the form of reality. Utilizing this tool is like affirming a dream *with gratitude* and doing it divinely, which is designed to help one become aware of proper guidance.

Once you are in the state of higher awareness, you must apply wisdom for a fool who fools on purpose is shown less mercy. Once you know better, do better! Be better. And no excuse, strive better! You will be moved organically to improve the more you do this with pure intent.

Prayer is good for utilizing the benefits of affirmation, which is simply to confirm your faith. Shy away from begging and pleading with thoughts of lack. You want to affirm with *gratitude* and claim what you want from the heart space where God is within you. You will come to find this is there all along in plain sight. Learn the art of getting up off your a**. Show gratitude for already having everything you need to succeed.

Affirm gratitude for your needs are already known.

When you're articulating your needs, it's very beneficial to learn *element bending*. What is element bending? How does it correlate with everyday success?

Element air is linked to your thought. You must articulate with your intelligence what you want.

Element fire is linked to visualization and the desire to see what you want in reality. What does what you want look like?

Element water is linked to how what you want and visualize make you feel inside. How it moves through you will be the result of the outcome. How does it make you feel?

Element earth deals will practicality. Now that you know what you want, how it looks, and how it makes you feel, you must apply the steps necessary to make it real.

This concept can also apply to any relationship you come across in life. How it starts off is how it will finish. This logic can be applied to man and woman coming together, and in general, with anything because sex is two minds coming together to create one mind. That mind is literally a baby, a new idea, new energy produced that forms afterward, or a literal new birth of something first imagined now into reality/dream/goal/new world, and so on. For example, the divine with the masculine and feminine energy correlate. See:

> *Air:* Thought—divine energy itself—a communicative thought if what one wants to achieve or receive. For example, prayer is you communicating what's on your mind and you use it to clearly affirm what you want. It's good to ask for the *ability/knowledge/the how to get it.*

> *Fire:* Visualization and desire, seeing what you want looks like. This is masculine because men are known to be more visually driven.

> *Water:* Water refers to prescient feelings and emotions about an outcome. It is also referred to as feminine intuition or gut feeling.

Earth: Practicality, the necessary steps that will lead to making it real. Now you see the birth creation of the feminine and masculine energies used in reality.

The point is, if we apply this to our everyday relationships, we will have more understanding of how to come together, whether it's in our professional or personal lives. For example, couples come together to create, cultivate with power and collective intention, and thus, create more generational wealth. The couple has a common interest that can stand through time as opposed to a man getting a lot of money just to get a female who has no real genuine interest in him, or the money is being spent outside of the needs of the collective household. Or a woman getting a lot of money just to spend years alone when she can come together with a man and form and work toward a collective goal. This is how we come together and change the world!

I'm not saying not to get your own money. Absolutely not. But coming together helps you get from taking the bus to taking the jet status!

These are all concepts you can apply regardless of background. They are general, effective, commonsense points you can use on any walk of life.

Following is a chart showcasing the seven energy centers of the body and their energetic vibrational meanings. It's good to use positive self-talk and self-affirmation to feed your mind nutrients, just as you feed your body. For example, when you speak negatively to plants, they die faster. But when you speak life, they sprout and grow. This was scientifically proven in a study of music vibrations and observing which ones kill and which heal.

Here's another example. Let's say you're craving McDonalds, which means it's on your mind. Whatever is on your mind consistently forms a vibrational rhythm. Now let's say that the whole time you're at work, you're saying, *I want McDonalds,* in the back of your mind. You know when you get off work you're going straight to McDonald's because it's been on your mind the entire time. A couple hours later, and you're at McDonalds. This is no coincidence. You attract things based on what is on your mind. It's the same as knowing what type of tree we're dealing with by the fruit it will bear. You said to your mind, *I want McDonald's,* and your mind took you to McDonald's.

Now, imagine you have clarity, wisdom, understanding, inner-standing, unity, love, compassion, riches, increase, wealth, abundance, prosperity, strength, peace, trust, guidance, honor, respect, faith, fitness, good health, healthy cravings, wellness, cleanliness, and so on in the back of your mind all day. What's going to happen? You will gain clarity, wisdom, understanding, inner-standing, unity, love, compassion, riches, increase, wealth, abundance, prosperity, strength, peace, trust, guidance, honor, respect, faith, fitness, good health, healthy cravings, wellness, and cleanliness! You can now see the powers that be and two ways to use it.

Just because you chanted all day doesn't mean the McDonald's will fall in your lap. It can come easily if you have someone around you who knows you like McDonald's. Maybe they just felt you wanted McDonald's, and the next thing you know, they brought you some McDonald's. You're shocked and think, *Wow! I was craving that all day. How did they know?* This is why identifying people who are aligned with your vibrations and having a pure intent to recognize those people is important.

Communicating something by thought and someone reacting to the vibrations of your thoughts is a form of telepathy, which is one of the original organic forms of language before language itself came about. Then the brain thought of itself to become brain. Without thought, it would have no name.

Let's go back to the McDonald's example. It took some tangible work for you to get there. You may have had to physically get in your car and drive to McDonald's. You can see that one way may have taken less work than the other. In one case, you had to physically go and get your McDonald's. But a different type of work is required if someone becomes attracted to and aware of your vibrations. If you form a clear thought of what you want and allow yourself to be open to receiving, someone else can bring it to you. Either way, this was a combination of faith and work. Faith with work leads you to your destination. Your faith is strengthened by getting a clear picture and articulating exactly what you want! It is important to have clarity to identify what it is so you do not overlook what has been presented to you.

Sometimes we don't see God because the source of God is hidden in plain sight. How nuts would it make someone to spend all his or her years searching for something already there? Searching is cute for beginners, but at some point, you must move up to the next level, which is observation. God is not the author of confusion, but merely exists in the wisdom of plain sight observation. Gratitude, which is confirming and being thankful for what you have observed—whether it be good or bad—and having clarity will set you free. This will lead to accumulation in the form of an epiphany, new horizons, opportunities, new levels of awareness, and spiritual or tangible results.

Be wise about the power of giving and receiving. Ask for proper guidance. How can you receive if you're afraid to give? How can you give if you're afraid to receive? Some women struggle with femininity and are cautious about receiving. Receiving involves allowing, and people must be wise about what they allow themselves to receive. Wise, not afraid. When one has a pure heart and pure intent, love will always win in the end. Perfect love will cast out all things unlike its nature. Remember to keep your heart as light as a feather. Be gentle as the dove but wise as a serpent. Be as direct as possible. Get to know yourself in order to understand your true desires, wants, and needs. A player should never play a game without expecting to be played, but repetition may lead to beating the game.

Coming to self-realization, picking up the controller in the first place, is a choice. In theory, this is orchestrating that we have free will and will often ask ourselves why we are here. Was this because we were somewhere else and need to return? Is this our home? How do we get back to knowledge of self with the ability to see God in plain sight? Being aware of your thoughts is very helpful. Utilize your intelligence to master them. People who come to realize they are going to pass away soon would be consciously aware of how they allow their thoughts to vibrate. They likely wouldn't want to die with negative thoughts in their minds.

A true leader will always point you back to your true self!

NOTE

NOTE

NOTE

NOTE

NOTE

NOTE

NOTE

NOTE

NOTE

NOTE

7 Center Energy Points Of The Body

Balanced ...

1. Crown Energy : (Just Above Head)
Divine Cosmic
Connection Enlightenment
2. Invisible Spiritual Eye :
(Forehead Center)
Clairvoyant, Intuition , Psychic Abilities
3. Throat : Healing , Communication
, Creativity , Expressive , Honest , Appreciative
4. Heart : Centred , Loving , Compassionate , Empathy ,
Non Judgmental ,Self-Love,Aware
5. Solar Plexus : Disciplined , Driven ,
Integrity , Respectful , Desire, WillPower, Vitality,
Power,Energy
6. Sacral : Passionate ,Creative , Intimacy,Sexuality
7. Root : Secure , Stability,Trusting, Grounding , Independent,
Survival

7 Centered Energy Points of The Body

1. Feelings of Disconnectedness
From The Divine & Others.
2. Confused , Lost , Busy Body,
Busy Minded , Stressed Out.
3. Overtalk Others , Criticize , Complain,
Timid to Express Oneself and Creativity.
4. Clingy, Guarded , Selfish Behaviour ,
Needy , Feeling Unfulfilled, Self Pitty, ColdHearted
, Judgemental.
5. Procrastination, Conniving, Bully Behaviour,
Push Over.
6. Lack Of Acknowledgement of Self Worth /
Low Self Worth , Shy, Withdrawn, Feelings of Guilt.
7. Unstable , Insecure , Prone to Sickness , Unhealthy Ego ,
Dependent /Codependency.

Following is an affirmative guide to getting back to your true self.

Reaffirming & Embodying The Energy Back Into Alignment

1. I Am Grateful For Divine Awareness ,
I Am Grateful For Harmony & Peace !
2. I Am Calm , I AM SOLUTIONARY ,
I Am Grateful For The Wisdom To Solving All Problems ,
In All Things I See Infinite Positive Possibilities ,
I Am Grateful For The Wisdom For Knowing and
Applying Divine Wisdom !
3. I Am Grateful I Can Express Myself Freely how I Truly Feel
, I am Grateful For The Ability To Communicate Well
With Others !
4. I am Grateful For Allowing Myself To Feel Love ,
I Forgive Myself, I Am Grateful For Giving and Receiving Love
5. I Am Powerful , I Can Move Mountains ,
I Always Aim For My Full Potential, I Am Confident,
I Am Organized , I Can Accomplish My Dreams ,
6.I Am The Controller of My Destiny I Am Grateful
for Infinite Ideas I Am Comfortable with my Sexuality
7. I Am Grounded I Am Safe I Am Divinely Protected
I Am Grateful For Feeling Secure with Myself Thoughts
and Emotions I Am Infinitely Provided For ! I Have All I Need!

You may go through many life experiences that result from self-realization. Tuning into the energy space of God is how you beat the odds. From my experience, pure silence helped me a lot, as did just plainly speaking and seeking my truth. Positive affirmations and high-frequency vibrational music are like baby food for the soul. Like how it feels when getting a nice Zen massage. In the end, pure intent will always win! The goal is to remember to return to your original home, which is often hidden in plain sight or within your AKASHIC records.

There are many powers that be, and one must learn to utilize them wisely. For example, there's power in your tongue, so it's wise to watch the words you speak. Asking for clarity and guidance doesn't hurt; it is common sense. Learn what things to say and which give you no value to say. You're always receiving what you put out. You speak great things, and great things come back to you. Period.

Following your heart will help solve many mysteries. Without knowledge of what's within, it's hard to comprehend what's without. Self-knowledge helps clear all fears and doubts because the soul is not fearful and has no limitations. Change is inevitable, and the inevitable is change. What you do unto others is done unto you! Not a single leaf falls without the universe knowing. Everything happens for a divine reason that we put the uni in verse! Rhythm and flow are in everything we know! What's more powerful than status and money? Brains and energy. Use them wisely!

What is your brain linked to? (Remember that to be linked is to be connected, so connect wisely.) Your intelligence!

What are your intelligence and energy linked to? Well, you can divine this for yourself. Let your soul guide you because it sometimes remembers better than you can in your physical body. You want to be what you want to attract because everything external is a mirror reflection of what's internal. So, for example, if your energy is linked to divine all-knowing of all possibilities (God), then that tree shall bear the fruit from which it was planted! If you study God, guess what? you're gonna run right into it! And God is what? Not the author of confusion, and a true leader will what? Always point back to you as who you are at the very core of your being—before you were given a thought form, a language, or any name or label period. Mind-blowing, right?

BUSINESS BONUS
ESSENTIALLY YOU WANT TO TRAIN YOUR MIND TO THINK BIG.

THINK OF A $20
PRODUCT OR SERVICE IDEA .
WHERE THERE'S DEMAND ,
AND YOU CAN SUPPLY.
AS YOU EXPAND , THINK OF
A PRODUCT OR SERVICE
IDEA THAT'S $1K … YOU HIT
YOUR FIRST 1K SALES THAT'S 1MILLION.

BUSINESS AWARENESS
• THE PEOPLE NEEDS? (DEMAND)
• HOW YOU CAN SOLVE THE
PROBLEM ? (SUPPLY)
•PROVIDE EXCELLENT
CUSTOMER SERVICE EXPERIENCE
•AWARE OF CASHFLOW
(PROFITS & EXPENSES)
•RESEARCH DEMOGRAPHICS
AND GEOGRAPHICS
(DATA)&(ANALYTICS)

START UP MONEY
SELF FINDING IS POSSIBLE
MAY REQUIRE MORE STRATEGIC
PLANNING. BUT FOR EXAMPLE
I SET UP A LEMONADE
STAND AND SELL THEM FOR
$20 A JUG I HIT MY FIRST
1K SALES THATS $20K

NUMBERS BOARD
$20 PRODUCT VS $1K PRODUCT

$20 PRODUCT/SERVICE ….
1K SALES= 20K
2K SALES =40K
5K SALES = 100K
10K SALES = 200K
1M SALES = 20M
20M SALES = 400M
400M SALES = 8BILLION
1B SALES = 20B
2B = 40B
3B = 60B
4B = 80B

$1K PRODUCT/SERVICE…
1K SALES = 1M
2K SALES = 2M
10K SALES = 10M
1M SALES = 1BILLION
20M SALES = 20BILLION
400M SALES = 400BILLION
1BILLION SALES = 1TRILLION

OTHER FUNDING OPTIONS
ARE OPENING UP
A LLC AND ESTABLISHING
BUSINESS CREDIT
/INC COMPANY
•GRANTS &
•INVESTORS
(RESEARCH
OR HAVE A PROFESSIONAL
PUT YOUR IDEA INTO
A BUSINESS BLUEPRINT)
•LEARN HOW TO PITCH
YOUR IDEA.
•DIRECT YOUR ATTENTION TO CREATING SYSTEMS
(STUDY SYSTEM BUILDING)
•FIND A PROFESSIONAL
FOR MARKETING /ADVERTISING CAMPAIGNS

IT'S 7+ BILLION
PEOPLE ON THE PLANET…
THERE ARE MANY
PRODUCTS AND SERVICES
PEOPLE PAY $20-1K
FOR (FIND OUT
WHAT YOUR PURPOSE IS
AND HOW YOU CAN EXECUTE)
I HOPE I INSPIRE YOU
WITH GOD ALL THINGS
ARE POSSIBLE
IN ALL REALMS OF REALITY !
BEYOND JUST THIS ONE !

MAYBE YOUR PURPOSE IS TO SERVE , THERE'S NOTHING WRONG WITH THAT …
BUT MAYBE YOU'RE PURPOSE IS TO LEAD ! THERE'S NOTHING WRONG WITH THAT !

Credits/Inspirations/Mentors

The 71 Spiritual Laws of Success; Jet Li; *Chicken Soup for the Soul; The Master Key; The Science of Getting Rich; Reallionaire: Nine Steps to Becoming Rich from the Inside Out.* Alan Watts, *Letting Go, Here & Now,* and *The Purpose of Life.*1

Printed in the United States
by Baker & Taylor Publisher Services